Mexico

| Author | Mary Jo Keller |
| Illustrator | Barb Lorseyedi |

EP073 ©Highsmith® Inc. 1996, 2003, 2007
W5527 State Road 106, P.O. Box 800
Fort Atkinson, WI 53538

Table of Contents

The Hands-on Heritage series has been designed to help you bring culture to life in your classroom! Look for the "For the Teacher" headings to find information to help you prepare for activities. Simply block out these sections when reproducing pages for student use.

Geography

Mexico is the northernmost country in Latin America. It lies just south of the United States, with the Rio Grande forming part of the border between the two countries. To the south, Mexico borders the countries of Belize and Guatamala. The Pacific Ocean forms Mexico's western border, while the Gulf of Mexico and the Carribbean Sea form its eastern borders.

More than two-thirds of Mexico consists of mountains and high, rolling plateaus. Two great mountain ranges extend along the coasts. They are called the Sierra Madre Occidental in the west and the Sierra Madre Oriental in the east. A series of volcanoes, known as the *Volcanic Axis*, extends across the southern portion of Mexico.

Project
Learn about the geography of Mexico by coloring a map.

Materials
- blank Mexico map
- Instructions for Coloring
- colored pencils (not crayons)
- black pen
- map of Mexico showing geographical features

Directions
1. Follow the Instructions for Coloring for the blank Mexico map. Use a geographical map of Mexico as a reference.

For the Teacher
1. Copy one Mexico map (page 5) per student.
2. Copy one Instructions for Coloring (page 4) per student.
3. Provide students with a geographical map of Mexico.

Instructions for Coloring

1. Draw in and color the river between Mexico and the United States blue. Label it *Rio Bravo del Norte*, its Mexican name.

2. Draw in and color the mountain range on the western coast brown and label it *Sierra Madre Occidental*. Draw in and color the mountain range on the east orange and label it *Sierra Madre Oriental*. Use the Glossary at the back of the book to see what the words "oriental" and "occidental" mean.

3. Color the area between the mountains green and label it *Plateau of Mexico*. This area is home to the majority of Mexican people, and it is the chief agricultural region. Add some cornstalks.

4. Mexico's three highest peaks, *Orizaba*, *Popocatépetl,* and *Ixtacihuatl*, are all volcanoes. *Paricutin* is another volcano. Label their locations and connect the volcanoes with a thick red line. This is the *Volcanic Axis*, a series of volcanoes that extends across the southern edge of the Plateau of Mexico. Many of these volcanoes are active! Draw some smoke coming out of the volcanoes.

5. Color the coastline along the *Gulf of Mexico* purple. The northern part of this region is dry and covered with low thorny bushes and trees. Draw a thorny bush. As you go south, rainfall increases. The southern-most portion is a tropical rain forest. Draw a big green tree.

6. Label and color the *Sierra Madre del Sur* yellow. The Aztecs found much of their gold in the eastern portion of this area. Draw a gold nugget. Look up the definition of the word "sur" in the Glossary.

7. Label and color the *Yucatán Peninsula* pink. This area is a low limestone plateau. Limestone dissolves in water. The great pits that formed in the limestone by rain became sacred wells of the Maya. Draw a well.

8. Locate and label the capital, *Ciudad de México* (Mexico City). Mark it with a big star.

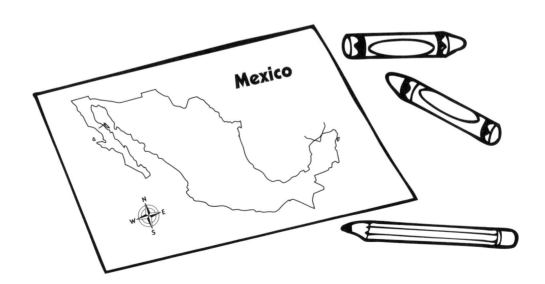

Mexico

Capital City

The flag of Mexico consists of three vertical stripes of green, white, and red. Green represents independence; white represents religion; and red represents union. In the center of the white stripe is the Mexican coat of arms, featuring an eagle perched on a cactus with a snake in its beak.

There is an interesting legend behind the coat of arms. The Aztec sun god told the ancient wandering Aztecs to end their nomadic lifestyle. They would find the location for their city when they saw an eagle eating a snake and sitting on a cactus bearing red, heart-shaped fruit. The Aztecs wandered for more than 150 years looking for the sign. They finally found the place their god had told them to settle. It was an island in swampy Lake Texcoco. They built the magnificent city of Tenochtitlán (tay-nawch-tee-TLAHN), which is now Mexico City, or Ciudad de México, the capital of Mexico.

Project

Make Mexican flags to learn about and understand Mexican tradition.

Materials

- Mexican Coat of Arms
- scissors
- tape
- crayons or colored pencils
- red and green construction paper

Directions

1. Color the Mexican Coat of Arms and cut the page along the dotted lines.
2. To assemble the flag, cut a piece of red and a piece of green construction paper the same size as the pattern page. Tape the construction paper to the edges of the pattern page, with the green on the left and the red on the right.

For the Teacher

Copy one Mexican Coat of Arms (page 7) per student.

EP073 Mexico © Highsmith® Inc. 2007

Mexican Coat of Arms

Early Mexico

The Indians of Middle America were the first farmers of the New World. As early as 5000 B.C., farmers began cultivating corn, beans, avocados, tomatoes, peppers, and squash. They raised turkeys for food as well. By 1500 B.C., people began settling in villages. And, without the need to constantly hunt for food, the people had time for arts, crafts, trade, and building. The Maya and Aztec became two of the most advanced civilizations in the Americas and helped lead to the development of Mexico.

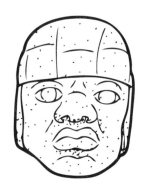

The Olmec—1200 B.C. to 200 B.C.

The first major civilization was the Olmec, which developed along the lowlands of eastern Mexico. The Olmec people built cities, established trade with other native groups, and developed a calendar and

a counting system. Sculptors carved massive stone heads as large as 9 feet (2.7 meters) tall and weighing as much as 15 tons! They may have worshiped a god that was part human and part jaguar. Jade figures and examples of beautiful pottery have been found in the ruins of an Olmec pyramid and ceremonial center at La Venta.

The Zapotecs—500 B.C. to A.D. 900

The Zapotecs lived in the eastern half of what is now the state of Oaxaca. They were fierce warriors and builders of great pyramids. To build their religious center at Monte Alban, Zapotec engineers and builders flattened an entire mountain top and pulled all the materials for the pyramids and temples up the sheer mountain wall! This advanced culture studied the stars and developed the first writing system in the Americas, using hieroglyphics (word pictures) to record their history on stone tablets.

The Maya—300 B.C. to A.D. 900

The Maya people built a magnificent civilization in southern Mexico as well as other parts of Central America. These native Americans produced remarkable architecture, sculpture, painting, and pottery. They devised a calendar more accurate than any used up to modern times. Mayan priests were both mathematicians and brilliant astronomers who were able to plot the course of the planet Venus with amazing accuracy.

The Aztec—A.D. 1200 to A.D. 1520

According to legend, the Aztec were instructed by their sun god to settle on an island in Lake Texcoco. By the 1400s, the mighty Aztec armies had built an empire that covered much of central and southern Mexico. There they built the magnificent island city of Tenochtitlán, home to 100,000 people! Its major streets were canals, which were spanned by drawbridges. At the center of the city rose massive pyramids topped with temples where thousands of human sacrifices were made.

EP073 Mexico © Highsmith® Inc. 2007

Ojo de Dios

Huichol Indians of present-day Mexico have kept many of their old traditions. Their dress, daily life, and religious ceremonies reflect a culture rich in folk art with a deep respect for nature.

The *Ojo de Dios*, or God's Eye, is a well-known religious symbol of the Huichol. They believe that the design of the eye has power to heal and protect. The Ojo de Dios is hung on the wall to be used in ceremonies and during prayer.

Project

Experience Huichol folk art by making an Ojo de Dios by wrapping colorful yarn around crossed sticks.

Materials

- yarn in several bright colors
- 2 sticks—twigs, craft sticks, dowels, or chopsticks, approximately 5 inches long
- scissors
- cardboard
- glue

Directions

1. Cross the two sticks and tie them together at the point where they cross with a strand of yarn. Do not cut off the yarn.

2. Wrap the yarn completely around one stick, then continue from stick to stick, wrapping the yarn completely around each one.

3. Tie on different-colored yarns as you go to create a bright pattern.

4. When you have reached the ends of the sticks, glue the end of the yarn to the end of the last stick.

5. Make tassels to hang from each point by wrapping yarn around a piece of cardboard. On one side, thread another piece of yarn underneath and tie the ends. Use scissors to cut the yarn on the opposite side. Tie a tassel to each point.

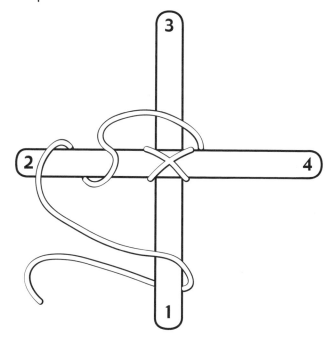

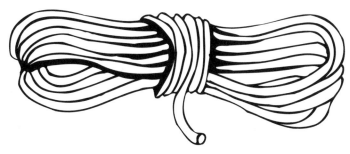

Aztec Writing

The Aztec people had no alphabet so they used *pictographs*, or little pictures, to represent words. For example, a picture of a foot meant "travel." Books were written by priests who were trained as *scribes*. The scribes primarily kept record books, but they also wrote books on history, religion, day-to-day living, and even poetry!

Aztec books were written on thin pieces of inner bark from fig trees. The pieces were varnished and stuck together to make long strips, some as long as 35 feet (11 meters)! The scribe would draw on both sides of the paper, making sure that he drew the important people larger than the others. The book was then folded like an accordion.

Project

Work as a cooperative group to make an Aztec manuscript.

Materials

- white paper
- pencils
- crayons
- tape

Directions

1. Turn your paper sideways with the long side on top.
2. Think of two stories: they can be something that happened to you, or something that you made up.
3. Use the examples below or create your own pictographs to sketch a general outline of your story. Remember to make the more important figures larger than the rest! Use a vertical line to end a sentence or thought. Draw one story on each side of the paper, then color.
4. Lay out everyone's papers on the floor, end to end. Tape together to make a long manuscript. Fold the book accordion-style when it is finished.

animal

night

day

house

sister, mother

brother, father

tree

campfire

bed, cot

tent

mountains

river

flower

bird

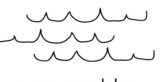
ocean, sea, lake

EP073 Mexico © Highsmith® Inc. 2007

Aztec Warriors

Aztec boys were trained to be warriors in a boarding school called a *telpuchcalli*. They learned to use the *maquahuitl*, a wooden sword edged with sharp pieces of volcanic glass. Warriors wore padded tunics and carried shields.

When a young warrior had taken three prisoners alive in battle, he was entitled to tie his hair up in a top knot and wear a feathered headdress.

Project

Make an Aztec feathered headdress.

Materials

- tagboard
- scissors
- stapler
- tape
- sequins, glitter, foil paper, etc.
- crayons or markers

Directions

1. Cut a crown shape from tagboard to fit around your head. Staple or tape the ends together.
2. Color the front side, using crayons or markers.
3. Glue on an assortment of decorations, including disks cut from foil, bits of feathers, etc.
4. Cut out and color construction-paper feathers.
5. Staple or glue the feathers onto the crown as shown.

Calendar

Mayan priests used their highly advanced studies of astronomy and mathematics to develop two kinds of calendars. One was a 260-day religious calendar, used for celebrations throughout the year. The days were named for different gods and goddesses. Priests used these calendars to predict good luck or bad luck.

The second type of calendar developed by the Maya was a solar calendar. It contained 365 days, like our modern calendar. Instead of 12 months, the Mayan calendar had 18 months with 20 days each. Five days remained at the end of the year. The Maya thought that these five days were extremely unlucky!

Project
Make and use a calendar that demonstrates how the Mayan calendar was used to name days.

Materials
- Calendar Patterns
- scissors
- colored pencils or crayons
- tagboard or cereal boxes
- brads
- toothpicks
- tape

Directions
1. Color the calendar circles. Glue the pattern to tagboard and cut out each circle.
2. Tape toothpicks to the back of the larger circle as shown. Make sure each toothpick lines up with an image on the front.

How to Use the Calendar
Notice how the wheels turn so that each day fits into a number. If you were to begin on 1 Rabbit, you would turn the wheels toward each other so that the next day would be 2 Water. When you get back to 1 again, you are starting a new cycle.

3. Use a brad to conect both circles to a piece of tagboard. Place the two circles next to each other so they barely touch, meeting like gears.
4. Practice using the calendar.

For the Teacher
Copy one Calendar Patterns (page 13) per student.

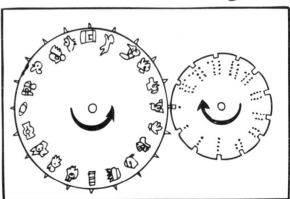

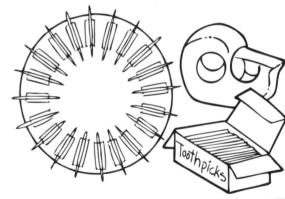

Calendar Patterns

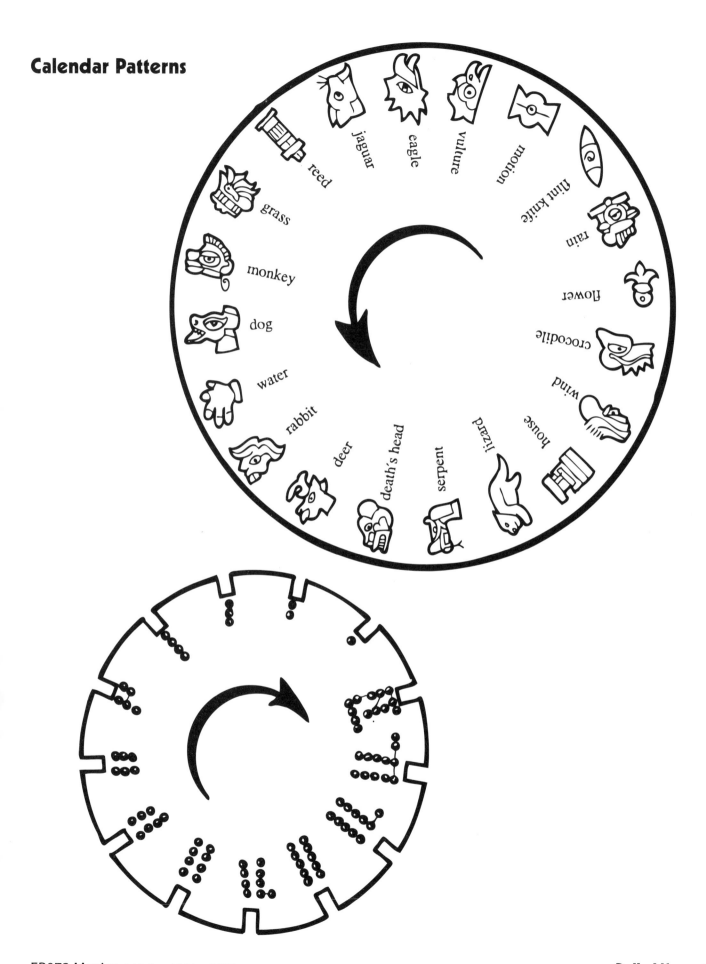

Village Life

In the small farm villages of Mexico, the village plaza is the center of the community. It is there that the church, government buildings, and shops are located.

The housing shapes and styles of the village vary according to the climate. In the dry central area of Mexico, the houses are made of adobe, a mixture of mud and clay that is formed into bricks and dried in the sun. In areas of heavy rainfall, houses have walls built of poles that have been coated with lime and clay. This process is more water-resistant than adobe.

Project
Make a classroom diorama of a Mexican village.

Materials
- 8 oz. (240 ml) milk containers
- penne pasta (long, thin tube pasta)
- tempera paint and paintbrushes
- white construction paper
- scissors
- Village Life Patterns
- brown butcher paper
- twigs, pebbles, sand
- tagboard scraps
- green tissue paper

Directions
1. Choose an area for the diorama and cover with brown paper.
2. Make houses, churches, and shops. Paint the house patterns to look like adobe. Once dry, cut them out. Glue the patterns to a milk carton. Have an adult cut the door and window along the solid lines.
3. Glue the pasta onto the roof. When the glue is dry, paint the roof red to look like red roof tiles. Add a tagboard steeple to the church.
4. Arrange the buildings in the village. Paint in roads and fields of crops. Crumpled pieces of green tissue paper make good cabbages for the field.
5. Add finishing touches to the village. Glue twigs to small rectangles of tagboard to make kitchen lean-tos for the houses. Pave the street in the plaza with cobblestones made from small pebbles glued closely together. Make dirt roads by the farms by spreading a thin layer of glue and sprinkling on sand.
6. Color the people and animals. Glue to tagboard and cut out. Fasten a small tagboard tab to the back of each figure so it stands upright. Arrange them in the village.

For the Teacher
Copy one Village Life Patterns (page 15) onto white construction paper per student.

Village Life Patterns

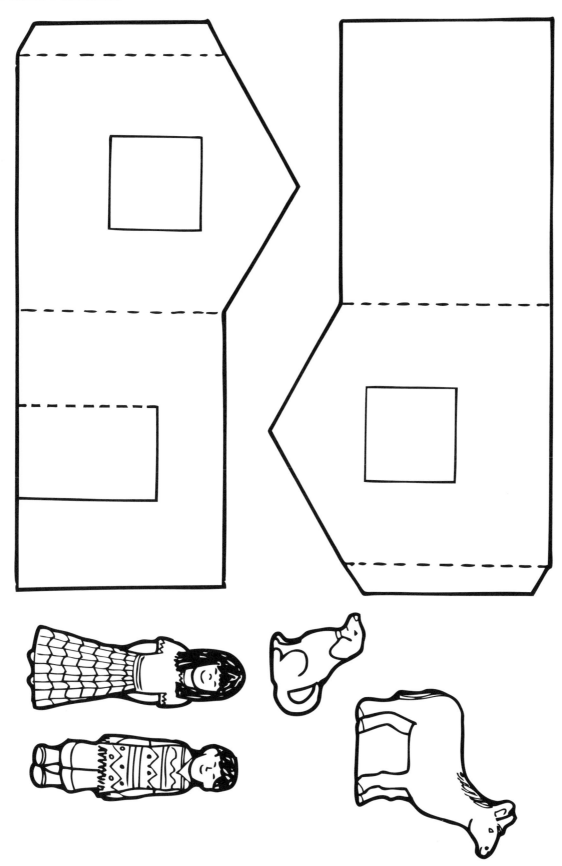

Marketplace

There is a marketplace in almost every village, city, and town in Mexico. Going to the market is a very popular activity, especially in the farm areas. People who wish to sell the items they have brought to the market can rent a stall if they wish or just spread their goods on the ground.

People bring items such as baskets, lace, produce, food, crafts, and pottery to sell or trade. The atmosphere in the marketplace is festive and noisy as people chat and visit with friends, and buyers and sellers bargain for the best deals.

Project

Learn how a marketplace functions by experiencing it firsthand!

Materials

- Small items brought from home to trade

Directions

1. With your parents' permission, bring a beach towel and a few small items from home to trade.

2. Push the desks to the side of the classroom. Spread your towel on the floor and arrange your items. Take turns browsing through the market and being a vendor. Items may be traded several times!

For the Teacher

Make sure your students have their parents' permission before participating in the Marketplace.

Rodeo

The northern portion of the Plateau of Mexico, known as the Mesa del Norte, was known for its huge cattle ranches. The ranch hands became skilled at riding and roping cattle, and soon they began having competitions. Roping, steer wrestling, and horsemanship were some of the events of these early competitions. The Mexican cowboys, or *vaqueros*, then organized Mexican-style rodeos, or *charreadas*. Later, American cowboys learned the skills of the Mexican vaqueros and organized their own competitions, known as *rodeos*.

The words "lariat," "lasso," "stampede," and "rodeo" are all words used in the United States that came from the Mexican "vaqueros."

Project

Learn a to tie a classic bowline knot.

Materials

- 15-foot (4.5 m) length piece of rope
- a target, such as a chair

Directions

1. Hold the rope vertically in your left hand. Use your right hand to cross the bottom of the rope over the top, creating a circle halfway up the rope.

2. Move just the very bottom rope end up through the circle, like a bunny peaking out of its hole.

3. Guide the rope end around the back of the top rope. This is the bunny running around the tree.

4. Then, the bunny jumps back in its hole, and you put the rope back through the loop, top to bottom.

5. Stand with your right shoulder facing the target. Swing the rope while you aim, then toss the rope and lasso your target.

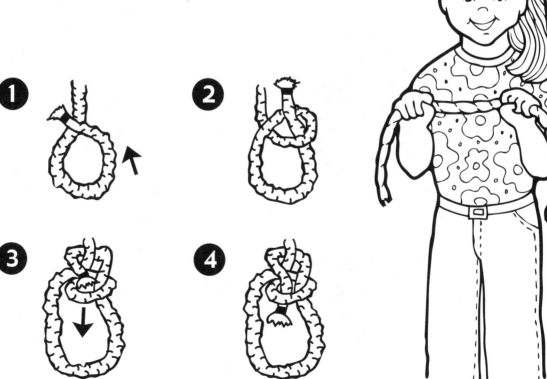

Quetzalcoatl

According to ancient legend, the Maya and Aztec god *Quetzalcoatl* once lived among the people of ancient Mexico. He is responsible for teaching them religion, art, culture, and agriculture. This gentle god told the people that human sacrifice was evil and that he preferred gifts of butterflies. Quetzalcoatl was driven out of Mexico by a rival god, but before he rode away on a winged serpent, he promised to return and rule Mexico.

Quetzalcoatl is represented as a feathered serpent and is associated with the planet Venus. Considered to be a great benefactor of mankind, Quetzalcoatl was the god of wisdom and knowledge.

Project

Use the style of ancient Mayan artists to color a picture of the Indian god Quetzalcoatl.

Materials

- Quetzalcoatl picture
- scissors
- crayons or markers

Directions

1. Color the picture of Quetzalcoatl in the style of ancient Mayan artists. Outline the figure in black, then color in with solid colors. Mayan artists rarely shaded the colors.

For the Teacher

Copy one Quetzalcoatl picture (page 19) per student.

Quetzalcoatl

Mexican Food

The Mexican diet of today is a blend of Indian and Spanish cooking, with some influence from French and Italian cuisine. The peasants developed most of the recipes, using ingredients easily available to them. Corn, chilies, tomatoes, and beans are the staples of the Mexican diet. Corn, for example, is ground into *masa* and set to make tortillas, or Mexican bread.

Project

Prepare Mexican dishes to taste, or as part of a fiesta (page 35).

Materials

See individual recipes for ingredients and materials to prepare each dish.

For the Teacher

If making tacos, prepare beef before class:

Heat olive oil in a frying pan over medium-high heat. Add ¾ lbs of beef, sliced into thin slices. Add 3 Tbsp. black pepper and 1 tsp. salt. Stir. Add ⅓ cup lime juice and 1 Tbsp. Worcestershire sauce. Let simmer for 5 minutes, stirring occasionally.

Guacamole is made from mashed avocados, which are native to Central America. Serve it with tortilla chips or as a sauce for other dishes.

- 2 large ripe avacados, peeled and pitted
- ½ tsp. (2.5 ml) salt
- 2 Tbsp. (30 ml) diced onion
- ½ tsp. (2.5 ml) garlic salt
- 2 Tbsp. (30 ml) olive oil
- 2 Tbsp. (30 ml) lemon or lime juice

Mash the avocados until smooth. Stir in remaining ingredients. Cover and refrigerate at least 1 hour before serving.

Rice is another staple in the Mexican diet.

- 1 onion, chopped
- 1 Tbsp. (15 ml) oil
- 1 cup (240 ml) uncooked rice
- 2⅓ cup (560 ml) beef broth
- 1 cup (240 ml) canned tomato puree

Cook onion in oil in electric skillet. Add uncooked rice and cook, stirring constantly, for a few minutes until rice begins to color. Add beef broth and canned tomato puree. Cover and cook about 25 minutes until rice is tender.

Tacos are a form of Mexican sandwich. They are folded tortillas that are filled with a variety of ingredients.

- warm corn tortillas
- diced cilantro
- diced onion
- hot sauce
- 1 lime, cut into wedges
- sliced beef, cooked in lime juice and Worcestershire sauce

Top one corn tortilla with a serving of meat. Top with cilantro and onion. Squeeze lime juice over the meat and add hot sauce if desired.

Beans, or **frijoles**, are as important in the Mexican diet as tortillas and, like them, are served throughout the day. Often, the beans are mashed and served as frijoles refritos (refried beans).

- 1 lb (450 g) dried pink or pinto beans
- 6 cups (1.5 L) water
- 1½ tsp. (7.5 ml) salt
- 2 Tbsp. (30 ml) bacon fat

Cover dried pink or pinto beans with water. Simmer over low heat for 12 hours. Add salt and bacon fat. Continue cooking until beans are tender.

EP073 Mexico © Highsmith® Inc. 2007

Mexican Recipes

Mexican soup is either liquid, *aguada*, or dry, *sopa seca*. A dry soup is like a casserole.

Pozole (Corn Chowder)

- ¾ cup (180 ml) chopped onion
- 1 small can chopped green chilies, drained
- 1 tsp. (5 ml) chili powder
- 1 Tbsp. (15 ml) oil
- 3 cups (750 ml) chicken broth
- 2 15 oz. (430 g) cans white hominy, drained

Saute onion, chilies, and chili powder in oil for 7 minutes. Add broth; simmer 30 minutes. Add hominy and cook another 30 minutes.

A nutritious drink enjoyed at the marketplace is called a **licuado**.

1½ cups (360 ml) milk

1 cup frozen strawberries

1 ripe banana, sliced

Combine milk, strawberries, and banana slices in blender. Blend until smooth. Makes about 2 servings.

Cacao was cultivated by the Indians long before the arrival of the Spanish. The Aztecs considered chocolate to be a special beverage and used cacao beans as a form of money. The Aztecs made their hot chocolate with water. Mexican cooks roast and grind the cacao beans at home! A molinillo is used to whip the hot chocolate until it foams.

- ¼ cup (60 ml) unsweetened cocoa
- ¼ cup (60 ml) sugar
- ¾ tsp. (4 ml) cinnamon
- salt
- 4 cups (950 ml) milk
- ½ cup (120 ml) half & half
- ¾ tsp. (4 ml) vanilla

Heat 1 cup milk in a saucepan until simmering. With a wisk, stir in cocoa, sugar, cinnamon, and salt. Turn up heat and bring to a boil, stirring constantly. Stir in remaining 3 cups of milk and return to a boil. Wisk until frothy. Add vanilla and half & half.

Mexican Wedding Cookies (**Polvorones**) are crumbly cookies that are baked for many traditional parties.

Preheat oven to 350° F (180° C). Combine:

- 2½ cups (590 ml) flour
- ¾ cup (180 ml) sifted powdered sugar
- 1 cup (240 ml) chopped pecans
- 2 tsp. (5 ml) vanilla
- 1 cup (240 ml) softened unsalted butter
- 1 tsp. (5 ml) cinnamon

Cream sugar and butter. Add flour, vanilla, cinnamon, and pecans. Kneed dough until all ingredients are incorporated. Chill for one hour. Shape into small balls and place 2 inches apart on greased cookie sheet. Flatten slightly with a spoon. Bake 15 minutes or until slightly browned. Roll in powdered sugar when cool. Makes about 30 cookies.

A favorite dessert is a custard pudding called **flan**. It is made of eggs, sugar, and milk with a caramelized sugar glaze. Packaged flan mix is available at the supermarket. Prepare according to package directions.

Language

When the Spanish first came to Mexico in 1517, the people of middle America spoke many different languages. As the Spanish and Indian cultures blended, the Spanish language spread. However, in certain areas the people continued to speak their own language and the ancient languages were preserved. In Mexico today, one can still hear the ancient Maya and Zapotec languages.

Today almost all Mexican people speak Spanish, which is the country's official language, in addition to their own tribal language.

Project
Play a matching game and learn some simple phrases in Spanish.

Materials
- Language Match-Up Game
- crayons
- construction paper
- scissors
- glue

Directions
1. Color and cut out the language cards.
2. Try to match up the Spanish language card with the English language card that says the same thing.
3. After matching the cards correctly, glue them next to each other on construction paper to make a reference sheet. Practice saying the new words you have learned with a friend.

For the Teacher
Copy one Language Match-up Game (page 23) per student.

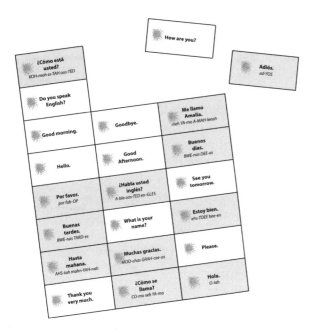

Answer Key

1.	Hola.	Hello.
2.	Buenos días.	Good morning.
3.	Buenas tardes.	Good afternoon.
4.	Adiós.	Goodbye.
5.	Hasta mañana.	See you tomorrow.
6.	Cómo se llama?	What is your name?
7.	Me llamo Amalia.	My name is Amalia.
8.	Por favor.	Please.
9.	Muchas gracias.	Thank you very much.
10.	¿Cómo está usted?	How are you?
11.	Estoy bien.	I am fine.
12.	¿Habla usted inglés?	Do you speak English?

Language Match-up Game

¿Cómo está usted? *KOH-moh es-TAH oos-TED*	How are you?	Adiós. *ad-YOS*
Do you speak English?	My name is Amalia.	I am fine.
Good morning.	Goodbye.	Me llamo Amalia. *meh YA-mo A-MAH-leeah*
Hello.	Good afternoon.	Buenos días. *BWE-nos DEE-as*
Por favor. *por fa-VOR*	¿Habla usted inglés? *A-bla oos-TED en-GLES*	See you tomorrow.
Buenas tardes. *BWE-nas TARD-es*	What is your name?	Estoy bien. *ehs-TOEE bee-en*
Hasta mañana. *AHS-tah mahn-YAH-nah*	Muchas gracias. *MOO-chas GRAH-cee-as*	Please.
Thank you very much.	¿Cómo se llama? *CO-mo seh YA-ma*	Hola. *O-lah*

Clothing

Most people in Mexico's larger cities and towns dress in Western-style clothing—like the clothing people wear in the United States and Canada. However, in small, isolated villages, people often wear the same type of clothing that was worn centuries ago. Women wear long, full skirts and white blouses. They will often cover their heads with *rebozos*, which are fringed shawls. Men wear simple white shirts and pants, along with sandals called *huaraches*. To shade themselves from the hot sun, they wear wide-brimmed hats known as *sombreros*.

Project

Make traditional pieces of Mexican clothing.

Materials

- Clothing Project Page
- material lists that accompany each clothing project.

For the Teacher

Copy one Clothing Project Page (25) per student. Bring in a sewing machine. Enlist parent volunteers to come in and help the students with the sewing.

Mayan Dress

The Mayan women of Yucatan wear long, loose white dresses that are embroidered around the neck and bottom hem.

Materials

- white T-shirt
- white sheet or fabric
- scissors
- crayons or permanent marker
- sewing machine

Directions

1. Cut a piece of fabric to make a fairly long skirt that will wrap around your waist 1½ times.

2. Color a design around the bottom of the fabric and around the neckline of the shirt. Press hard on the crayons to get a bright color or use permanent marker.

3. Have an adult help you sew the skirt closed down the side. Then, fold over the top of the fabric about 2 inches (5 cm) and sew, leaving an opening to insert elastic.

4. Cut a piece of elastic to fit around the waist. Insert into casing and secure with a few hand stitches, bunching the fabric to create a very loose, flowing skirt.

Clothing Project Page

Sombrero

A *sombrero* is a wide-brimmed hat made of felt or straw that is worn as protection from the hot sun. The men's national costume—a dark blue *charro* suit, which consists of a short bolero jacket and riding pants with gold or silver buttons down the sides, a flowing red bow tie, and spurred boots—is topped with a fancy white sombrero.

Materials

- heavy duty paper bowl
- tagboard
- glue
- scissors
- pencil
- paintbrushes
- yarn or string
- compass
- tempera paint

Directions

1. Cut a large circle from tagboard—about 2 feet (61 cm) in diameter.

2. Use a compass to draw a circle in the center of the tagboard that is slightly smaller than the diameter of the paper bowl. This is your cutting line.

3. Cut out the circle and glue the bowl to the large circle as shown. Paint your sombrero to look like straw or felt.

4. Poke two holes in the brim. Cut a long piece of yarn or string. Thread it through both holes so it can be tied under the chin.

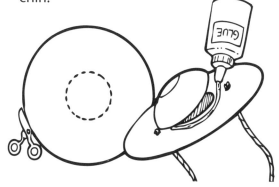

Poncho

During the cold or rainy weather, a man might wear the traditional *poncho,* which is a blanket that has a slit in the center for the head to go through.

Materials

- white sheet or muslin, cut in a 4 x 4 foot (1.2 m) square
- crayons
- scissors

Directions

1. Color bold designs onto the muslin square, including different-colored stripes.

2. Cut a slit in the center for your head to fit through.

To complete this traditional costume, wear white pants or jeans and a white dress shirt and wear sandals.

Folk Art

The work created by artists who have had no formal art training is called *folk art*. These beautiful carvings, needlework, decorative items, and paintings are rarely signed by the artist and can be found in marketplaces throughout the world.

Modern Mexican folk art is rich in tradition. The beauty and variety of Mexican crafts can be found in the delicate feathered mosaics and tiny masks of jade, rock crystal, and turquoise carved by the early Indians. The wrought iron and gold work of the colonial period, and the beautifully decorated pottery and textiles of today are other examples of the folk art for which Mexico is famous throughout the world.

Project

Plan a day to make Mexican folk art examples.

Materials

- Folk Arts Project Page
- individual material lists for each craft

Directions

1. Divide into the groups your teacher has assigned.
2. Rotate through the craft stations as scheduled by your teacher. Complete each craft at the station by following the directions.

For the Teacher

1. Set up craft centers in the classroom. Stock each with a copy of the Folk Arts Project Pages (26 and 27) and materials for one of the crafts described.
2. Ask parent volunteers to help at each center.
3. Divide class into groups. Develop a rotational schedule so that each group has time at each center.
4. Allow time at the end of the day to share what was learned.

Mexican Mirror Plate

Brightly colored yarn is used in a variety of ways by Mexican folk artists. They create beautiful "paintings" by filling in the outline of their design with colorful yarns. Yarn is also used to add decoration to items such as this mirror.

Materials

- cardboard
- aluminum foil
- glue
- yarn, assorted thicknesses and colors
- scissors
- crayons

Directions

1. Cut cardboard into an oval. Glue a large piece of aluminum foil into the center of the cardboard.
2. Draw a design on the cardboard with crayons, leaving an oval shaped section of foil exposed in the center.
3. Fill in your design with colored yarn. Spread a thin layer of glue ahead of the yarn, then press the yarn in place.

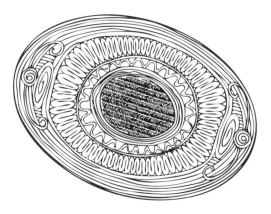

Folk Arts Project Page

Bark Painting

Bark painting is a Mexican folk art that has its roots in ancient times. Early Central-American Indians stripped the bark from amate or wild fig trees to use as paper. Their paint was a mixture of powdered minerals mixed with plant juice.

Materials

- brown paper bags
- tempera paints
- paintbrushes
- pencils
- scissors

Directions

1. Cut the paper bag to size.
2. Draw a design such as an animal or plant, the most common themes of modern bark painting.
3. Paint in the design, leaving the background unpainted to show the "bark."

Tin Lantern

Mexican folk artists use tin to make crowns, mirror frames, and other decorative items such as candle holders. These festive candle holders may be set on a table or hung from the ceiling. When many candle holders are hung from the ceiling at different heights, the candlelight shining out from the holes makes beautiful flickering patterns on the walls and ceilings.

Materials

- clean, empty tin cans
- pencil
- big nails
- permanent markers
- tape
- paper
- hammer
- scissors

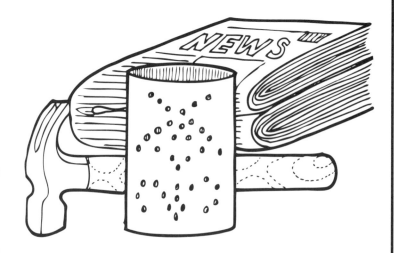

Directions

1. Cut paper to fit around a tin can. Draw a pattern of dots onto the paper and tape paper to the can.
2. Fill the can with water and freeze.
3. Once frozen, use a hammer and nail to punch holes through the dots you drew.
4. Remove the paper and allow the ice to melt.
5. Color the tin can with permanent markers.

Murals

Mural painting is a Mexican art form that dates back to ancient times. Mayan murals were first painted on temple walls in A.D. 700. During the Spanish colonial period, artists painted beautiful murals in churches.

In the 1900s, artists such as Diego Rivera, David Siqueiros, and José Orozco created powerful murals that were vivid in color and bold in design. Their work can be seen in many public buildings. These famous mural artists painted scenes from Mexican history. Many of the murals tell stories about the peasant and worker revolutions.

Project
Paint a classroom mural in the style of the famous Mexican mural painters.

Materials
- white butcher paper
- pencils
- tempera paint
- paintbrushes
- slide projector (optional)

Directions
1. Work with your classmates to design a mural. Use a pencil to draw the design, covering the butcher paper on the wall. Choose an event that actually happened in Mexico or in your community for your mural's subject. Or, use a pencil to trace the design that is being projected onto the butcher paper.
2. Paint the design with brightly colored tempera paints.

For the Teacher
1. Cover a wall with white butcher paper.
2. You may choose to project an image onto the paper for your students to paint, or you may let them decide the mural's design.

Lacquerware

Lacquer work in Mexico dates back to pre-Columbian times. Artisans of this period applied lacquer, a type of varnish, to the surface of wooden utensils for two reasons. Not only did the lacquer seal the wood and make it impervious to high temperatures and moisture, but it gave the object a rich, decorative sheen.

The two basic types of lacquer work found in Mexico today are an etched variety and a painted type that is used to decorate trays, bowls, and dishes.

Project
Create a plate that resembles Mexican lacquerware.

Materials
- heavy duty paper plates
- tempera paint
- pencil
- paintbrushes
- spray-on sealer (ex. Krylon™)

Directions
1. Paint both sides of the plate with dark blue, green, or black paint. Let dry.
2. Paint a red stripe around the edge of the plate. Let dry.
3. Use the pencil to draw a design such as a bird, tree, or flower onto the plate. Paint the design with bright, strong colors. Let dry.

4. When completely dry, spray the plate with the spray-on sealer, which is a kind of lacquer, to give the plate the sheen of lacquerware.

For the Teacher
Only use the spray-on sealer in a well-ventilated area.

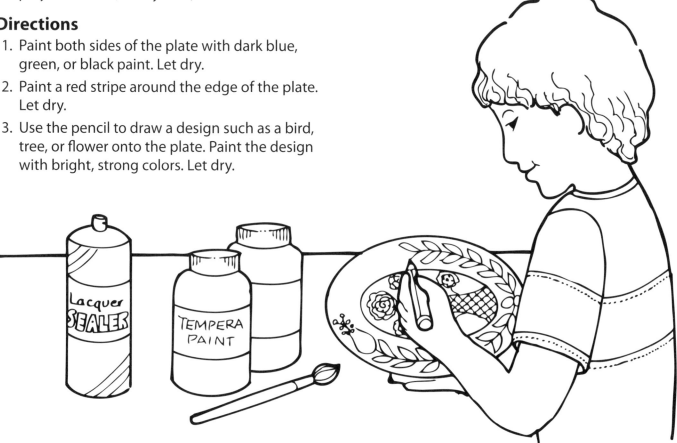

Games

Many ancient religious centers throughout Mexico had a special playing court for the game *tlachtli*, a kind of basketball. Only nobles were allowed to play this dangerous game that was also a type of religious ceremony. The losing team was sometimes sacrificed after the game to keep the gods happy!

In the late nineteenth century, the Spanish introduced a handball game played with basket-like racquets called *cestas*. This game is still being played in Mexico today in much the same form. Bullfighting was also introduced to Mexico by the Spanish, and remains a popular spectator sport to this day.

Soccer, baseball, basketball, golf, volleyball, and tennis are just a few other sports enjoyed in Mexico today.

Project

Explore Mexican culture with a day of games from Mexico's past and present.

Materials

Individual material lists for each game.

Ancient Games

Tlachtli

Tlachtli was a game similar to basketball. Players tried to hit a rubber ball through a stone ring high on a wall without using their hands!

Materials:

- Hula Hoop™
- basketball
- duct tape

Tape a hula hoop to a pole. Hold your hands together behind your back. Then try to hit the ball through the hoop using only your hips, elbows, or knees.

Modern Sports

Jai Alai

Jai Alai is known as the fastest game in the world. Players, wearing a glove with a long wicker basket attached, slam a hard rubber ball against a high wall. The ball may travel at speeds over 155 miles per hour!

Materials

- tennis rackets
- tennis ball
- high wall

Find a partner and take turns hitting the tennis ball against the wall. The server gets a point if the opponent misses a shot. Six points wins a game.

Soccer

Soccer is Mexico's most popular sport. Mexican soccer players are among the best in the world.

Materials

- soccer ball
- chalk
- field or playground

Divide players into two teams. Mark goal lines with chalk. Players try to kick the ball across their goal line. No hands allowed!

Bullfighting

Before some bullfights, the bulls are allowed to run through the streets. People run in front of the bulls or try to fight them as if they were matadors (bullfighters) in the ring!

Play a game of tag where the person who is "it" pretends to be a bull. The fun of this game is there can be more than one person who is "it"! When a player is tagged, he or she becomes a bull also.

Music and Song

Traditional music can be heard at fiestas throughout Mexico. *Mariachi* bands consist of four to 10 musicians. The members often wear sombreros and dress in uniforms trimmed with silver sequins. Violins, trumpets, and guitars are the most common instruments used in mariachi bands. Often, all of the members sing and play while they stroll through the streets.

Ranchera music is another popular type of Mexican music. It is common in rural areas and is often about everyday life. *Norteña* is a music genre associated with the people that live along the border between Mexico and the United States. It is a highly energetic music that deals with the stories of life along the border.

Project
Explore traditional Mexican music with a variety of activities.

Materials
- recordings of mariachi music, country-western music, or other folk music
- pencils

Directions
Follow the directions to hear, sing, and play traditional Mexican music.

For the Teacher
Gather examples of Mexican music to present to the class.

Sing It!
The famous folk song *"La Cucaracha"* (*"The Cockroach"*) was sung during the Mexican Revolution. In some of the verses, the soldiers make fun of their leader, Pancho Villa.

Everyone knows the tune to "La Cucaracha"—practice singing it in Spanish!

La cucaracha, la cucaracha, ya no puede caminar.

Porque no tiene, porque le falta, la patita principal.

Hear It!
There is usually a singer-leader, two horn players, two guitarists, and a bass player in a mariachi band.

Listen to a recording of mariachi music. Can you hear all the instruments?

Call out "Ay-ay-ay-ay" at the sad parts.

Play It!
Ranchera music is often compared to American country-western music.

Listen to a recording of country-western music or folk music. Play along by tapping on your desks with pencils.

Make your face match the music!

Dance

Mexico's folk dances are some of the most beautiful and varied dances in the world. Many dance troops today still perform the ancient Mayan and Aztec dances. The colorful costumes of the Conchero dancers include headdresses that are plumed with feathers more than 2 feet long! The dancers move in a slow, circular pattern. Tied to the wrists and ankles of some dancers are bracelets with tiny jingling bells attached to them.

El jarabe tapatío, or the Mexican hat dance, is a lively dance with hopping steps and heel-and-toe tapping. This popular folk dance is performed everywhere from village fiestas to the Palace of Fine Arts in Mexico City, where it is danced regularly by the Ballet Folklórico.

Project

Dance el jarabe tapatío, or the Mexican hat dance.

Materials

- music to the Mexican hat dance

Directions

Hop from foot to foot while the music is playing, clapping twice in between bars. Have fun swinging your partner during the refrain!

For the Teacher

1. Plan time to dance El jarabe tapatío, or make it an activity at a classroom fiesta.
2. Move the desks to the edges of the room to allow your students space to dance.

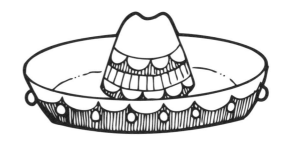

Weaving

Hand weaving is an ancient Indian art, and Mexican weavers are famous for their beautiful home-woven fabrics. Throughout Mexico, men wear colorful *serapes*, which are blankets worn over one shoulder. Because the styles of weaving vary in different parts of Mexico, the colors and designs woven into a serape tell where in Mexico it was made.

Belt-loom weaving is a traditional Mayan method of weaving that dates back hundreds of years and is still in use. One end of the loom is tied to the weaver's waist and the other end is tied to a tree or fence. Weavers create beautiful strips of fabric on these simple looms.

Project

Learn a simple type of weaving to make a colorful belt.

Materials

- heavy yarn in two bright colors
- scissors
- pencil

Directions

1. Cut a piece of yarn long enough to go around your waist twice. Use that piece of yarn to measure and cut 10 to 20 additional pieces of colored yarn, depending on how wide you want your belt to be.

2. Tie the yarn strands onto the pencil, leaving ends long enough to make a fringe (see illustration). Tie the ends together and fasten to the back of a chair or doorknob.

3. Start with the piece of yarn on the left and weave it over and under until it comes out on the right side. Take the next piece of yarn on the left and weave it over and under. Always start on the left and follow the over and under pattern. Keep the yarn even and straight, remembering not to pull too tightly.

4. When you are finished, knot the end and slide the pencil out of the loops.

EP073 Mexico © Highsmith® Inc. 2007

Fiesta

At a party you will always find good food and music! A party in Mexico is called a *fiesta*, and there are many fiestas throughout the year. People find many reasons to celebrate. One of the most lavish Mexican celebrations is the *quinceanera*. When a girl turns 15, her family throws her an elaborate party to celebrate her maturity. The party looks almost like a wedding: there is music, dancing, food, and decorations. The birthday girl usually dresses in a fancy white gown—almost like a wedding dress!

There are also many national, religious, and patriotic festivals throughout the year. In addition, each town honors their patron saint or a special event in their history with an annual fiesta.

Project

Work in cooperative groups to plan and carry out a Mexican fiesta.

Materials

- recipes
- cooking utensils and ingredients for selected recipes
- plastic utensils
- paper bowls, plates, and napkins
- butcher paper
- crayons or markers
- decorations such as a piñata, papel picado, or cascarones
- recording of Mexican Mariachi music

Directions

1. Divide into your group, as assigned by your teacher. Use the directions given to create some decorations for your fiesta.
2. On fiesta day, use the directions assigned to your group to prepare food for the fiesta.
3. Once the food is made, it is time to eat, mingle, play games, and have fun!

For the Teacher

1. Divide the class into groups.
2. Review the recipes in the Mexican Food section (pages 20–21) and assign responsibilities to each group.
3. Make copies of the cascarone (page 37), papel picado (page 40), and piñata (page 41) directions and assign projects to the groups.
4. Arrange for parent help on fiesta day. Assign table setters and servers.
5. During the week prior to fiesta day, have your students start making the decorations.
6. On fiesta day, set up areas where each group will prepare its contribution to the feast.
7. Play mariachi music to set the mood.

Masks

Masks are frequently worn at fiestas, ceremonial celebrations, dance performances, and theater productions in Mexico. The masks may be made from wood, papier-mâché, cloth, and gourds. Often the masks are made to symbolize different creatures from the animal world.

Mask-making in Mexico has a long history. The ancient Maya carved small detailed masks from rock, crystal, and marble. Mask makers of the Olmec tribe made masks in the image of their god who was part man and part jaguar. High ranking Aztec warriors wore wooden mask-like headdresses carved to look like eagles or jaguars.

Project
Make a mask using a variety of craft materials.

Materials
- heavy duty paper plates or platters
- tagboard
- paper bags
- scissors
- stapler
- yarn or string
- paint and paintbrushes
- variety of art materials such as:
  - colored construction paper
  - sequins
  - raffia
  - foam meat trays
  - egg carton sections
  - chenille sticks
  - pom-poms
  - feathers
  - rickrack

Directions
1. Choose to build your mask on a paper plate, paper bag, or tagboard shape.
2. Use your imagination and the available art materials to decorate your mask as you choose.
3. When complete, staple a piece of yarn on each side of your mask. Tie the yarn together behind your head to wear the mask.

For the Teacher
Set out the available art materials and let your students use their imaginations to create unique masks.

EP073 Mexico © Highsmith® Inc. 2007

Cinco de Mayo

The national holiday *Cinco de Mayo*, which means the 5th of May, commemorates the Battle of Puebla, which took place on that date in 1862. It was during this battle that untrained Mexican forces defeated an army of French mercenaries.

Cinco de Mayo is celebrated with boisterous fiestas throughout Mexico. In Mexico City, the president makes a stirring speech that is followed by a huge military parade through the streets of the capital.

Local celebrations include mariachi bands, ferris wheels, fireworks, dancing, and lots of delicious food and drink!

Project

Celebrate Cinco de mayo with a classroom fiesta. Make *cascarones* to have at your fiesta. Make sure you have a broom nearby!

Materials

- empty egg shells
- tissue paper
- scissors
- confetti
- tempera paint
- paintbrushes
- small funnel

Directions

1. Your teacher will provide you with an empty egg shell. Use a small funnel to fill the egg with confetti.
2. Glue a small piece of tissue paper over the opening to seal the confetti inside.
3. Paint the egg with bright colors.

For the Teacher

Teach students how, or empty a raw egg for each student in your class. Carefully use a large sewing needle to pierce a raw egg on both ends. Use scissors to expand the hole on one end. Hold the egg over a bowl and blow into the needle hole. The bowl will catch the raw egg. Rinse the egg and allow to dry thoroughly.

Día de la Raza

Día de la Raza (Day of the Race) is a very important national holiday in Mexico. On this day, the Mexican people celebrate their mixture of people, races, and cultures with pride. Columbus Day, October 12, is the day chosen for this celebration, as Cristóbal Colón, as he is called in Spanish, symbolizes the birth of the Mexican race.

It was Columbus who opened the way for the Spanish to come to middle America. Once there, the Spanish settlers married the native people and created a new race called *mestizos*. Today, seven out of 10 Mexicans are mestizos.

Project

Celebrate the different ethnicity of the students in your class with a sharing day.

Materials

- items or photographs brought from home

Directions

1. Bring in a photograph or an item that tells something about your family's ethnic background. Write a paragraph telling the history of the item you brought to show.

2. Present your item to the class.

For the Teacher

Give each student time to share his or her family's history during your class's own Día de la Raza.

EP073 Mexico © Highsmith® Inc. 2007

Día de los Muertos

On October 31, people in Mexico begin a three-day festival known as *Día de los Muertos* (Day of the Dead). It is believed that the spirits of deceased relatives and friends visit during these three days. On the first day, photographs, mugs of hot chocolate, candles, and sugar skulls are placed on an altar to invite the angelitos, or spirits of deceased children, to come back for a visit.

The following two days honor adult relatives and friends. November 1 is a day of visiting and feasting. The large altar is arranged with loaves of bread, flowers, fruit, and the relatives' favorite foods. Candles are lit, and fireworks signal the spirits' jouney home. For the next 24 hours the church bells ring continuously.

November 2, the last day of the celebration, is marked with a trip to the cemetery to bring flowers, enjoy a picnic, and visit. Some families even prepare their alter at the family grave site.

Project
Bake Pan de Muertos, a special sweet bread made for Día de los Muertos.

Materials
- 1 loaf frozen bread dough
- flour
- cookie sheet
- oven mitts
- knife
- 1 cup (240 ml) confectioners' sugar
- sifter
- 1 tsp. (5 ml) lemon juice
- 3–4 tsp. (15–20 ml) hot water
- colored sugar

Directions
1. Let the dough rise, following the label directions, until it has doubled in volume. Punch down and turn onto a lightly floured surface.

2. Cut off a small piece of dough for decoration and set aside. Shape the remaining dough into a round loaf.

3. Roll the reserved dough into a long thin rope. Lay it on top of the bread in the shape of a flower, moistening it slightly if necessary.

4. Let the dough rise in a warm place until doubled in bulk, about 1 hour.

5. Bake at 350° F (180° C) for 30–35 minutes.

6. Make icing while the bread is cooling. Mix sifted confectioners' sugar and lemon juice with hot water. Drizzle over bread in small loops. Sprinkle with multi-colored sugar.

For the Teacher
Assist students in cutting the dough.

Papel Picado

Papel picado, or punched paper, is a traditional folk art in Mexico that dates back to pre-Columbian times. This delicate paper craft is usually created to decorate an area where a festival will take place. On El día de los Muertos (Day of the Dead), families set up *ofrendas*, or alters, to celebrate the visit of deceased relatives. These tables are often decorated with strings of papel picado.

The designs of papel picado may be very simple or so intricate that a special paper chisel must be used to cut the design.

Project

Decorate the classroom with *papel picado*.

Materials

- brightly colored tissue paper
- scissors
- glue stick
- string

Directions

1. Layer several sheets of tissue paper. Draw a design on the top sheet.
2. Cut out the design—make sure you cut through all the layers of tissue paper at once.
3. Stretch string all around the classroom. Glue the papel picado to the string—fill the entire length!

EP073 Mexico © Highsmith® Inc. 2007

Piñata

Piñatas are containers made of earthenware or papier mâché. Many are shaped liked animals, most commonly dogs or donkeys.

The piñata is filled with candy, fruit, and toys. It is hung above the heads of the children from the ceiling or a tree. The children are blindfolded, and each gets a turn to try to hit the piñata with a stick until it breaks and showers down treats!

Piñatas are a favorite treat at fiestas and are part of many Mexican celebrations.

Project
Make a sun piñata and play the piñata game.

Materials
- large round balloon
- newspaper or paper towels
- 1 pint (480 ml) white glue
- tempera paint
- paintbrush
- yellow construction paper
- colored streamers or tissue paper
- sturdy string or twine
- small candies
- blindfold
- broom

Directions
1. Inflate a balloon and tie the end. Tear the newspaper or paper toweling into small pieces. Combine equal parts glue and water in a large disposable container.
2. Dip the paper pieces in the glue and cover the balloon with several layers of paper. Let dry.
3. Cut a hole in the top of the piñata and remove the balloon. Paint the piñata yellow. When the paint dries, add a smiling sun face. Make cones from yellow construction paper and hang streamers from the ends. Glue to the piñata to make the sun's rays.
4. Poke two holes at the top of the piñata. Attach string to make a handle for hanging.

For the Teacher
Once the piñata is complete, you may decide to use it. Fill it with candy and hang in an open space. Let your students take turns being blindfolded and trying to break the piñata with a broom handle. Make sure to keep your other students a safe distance away!

Las Posadas

People have been celebrating Las Posadas since it was introduced to Mexico by Fray Diego de Soria in 1587. On the nine nights before Christmas, friends and neighbors gather to recreate the Biblical story of the journey of Mary and Joseph to Bethlehem and their search for lodging on the night of Jesus's birth. These ceremonies are called *posadas*, which means shelters or lodgings.

With lighted candles, the procession of children and adults goes from house to house where shelter is denied. Finally they come to a home where they are welcomed with refreshments and a piñata for the children.

Project
Participate in the custom of Las Posadas by traveling to other classrooms looking for shelter.

Materials
- Las Posadas verses
- traditional costumes
- hot chocolate
- polvorones
- piñata
- candy to fill the piñata
- cups and napkins

Directions
1. Your teacher will direct you to three classrooms. At the first classroom, knock at the door and call out the first verse of Las Posadas. The teacher and class will respond with the second verse.

2. At the second classroom, again knock on the door and call out the first verse. The teacher and class will respond with the second verse.

3. At the third classroom, knock at the door and call out the third verse. The teacher and class will respond with the fourth. Answer with the fifth verse and they will respond with the sixth and seventh verses.

4. Enter the last classroom to enjoy refreshments and a piñata.

For the Teacher
1. Arrange with three other teachers to visit their classrooms. Plan for refreshments and a piñata to be at the last classroom.

2. Copy one Las Posadas verses page (43) per student, as well as enough copies for the teachers of the three classrooms you will be visiting. Encourage your students to dress in traditional costumes.

EP073 Mexico © Highsmith® Inc. 2007

Las Posadas

Spanish

Peregrinos:
En nombre del cielo
Os pido posada,
Pues no puede andar,
Mi esposa amada.

Posadero:
Aquí no es mesón
Sigan adelante,
Yo no puedo abrir,
No sea algún tunante.

Peregrinos:
Posada le pide,
amado casero,
Por sólo una noche,
La Reina del Cielo.

Posadero:
Pues si es una reina,
Quien lo solicita,
¿Cómo es que de noche,
Anda tan solita?

Peregrinos:
Mi esposa es María,
Es Reina del Cielo,
Y madre va a ser,
Del Divino Verbo.

Posadero:
¿Es usted José?
¿Su esposa es Maria?
Entren peregrinos.
No los conocía.

Entren santos peregrinos,
Reciban este rincón,
Que aunque es pobre la morada,
Se la doy de corazon.

English

Pilgrims:
In the name of heaven,
I ask you for lodging.
My beloved wife
Can no longer go on.

Innkeeper:
This is not a hotel.
Go on ahead.
I can't open the door,
You may be bad people.

Pilgrims:
Lodging I ask of you,
Friend innkeeper,
For just one night,
For the Queen of Heaven.

Innkeeper:
Well, if she's a queen
Who asks for it,
How come she travels
Alone at night?

Pilgrims:
My wife is Mary,
She is Queen of Heaven,
And she is going to be the mother
Of the Holy Child.

Innkeeper:
Are you Joseph?
Is your wife Mary?
Come in pilgrims.
I did not know who you were.

Come in holy travelers,
Take this corner in the stable.
Even though this place is poor,
I give it to you with all of my heart.

Guadalupe Day

Guadalupe Day, December 12, is the most important religious holiday in Mexico. People travel from all parts of Mexico to visit the chapel on Tepeyac Hill in Mexico City. It is believed that the mother of Jesus appeared there to an Indian peasant named Juan Diego.

The festivities include dance performances and parties. Throughout Guadalupe Day, people come to the church to pray and offer thanks for the cures of diseases and handicaps. Many of them pin small silver or tin objects that are shaped like hearts, arms, or legs near the statue of the Virgin of Guadalupe. These small religious charms are called *milagros* (miracles) and symbolize the giver's appreciation for a cure.

Project

Make paper roses and tin ornaments to celebrate Guadalupe Day.

Materials

See the material list on the assigned project.

Directions

1. Celebrate Guadalupe Day with a fiesta that includes making paper flowers and milagros.
2. Follow the directions for the project assigned to you by your teacher.

For the Teacher

Copy one Guadalupe Day Project Page (45). Assign one of the projects to each student.

The Story of the Virgin of Guadalupe

Mexicans believe that in 1531, Mary, the mother of Jesus, appeared to an Indian named Juan Diego. She asked Juan to go to the bishop and request that a church be built on the hill so she could be close to her people. When the bishop asked for a sign that the woman was indeed the Blessed Virgin, Juan opened his cape to show the roses that had sprung up at the site where roses had never grown before. But the bishop did not look at the roses. He gazed instead at the picture on the inside of the cape of the woman who had appeared to Juan. No one could explain how it got there! Juan's cape still hangs in the church built there.

EP073 Mexico © Highsmith® Inc. 2007

Guadalupe Day Project Page

Paper Roses

Materials
- red tissue or crepe paper
- green construction paper
- pipe cleaners
- scissors
- tape or glue

Directions
1. Cut crepe paper into 10-inch (25.4 cm) squares.
2. Lay 10–12 sheets on top of each other and fold acordian-style. Wrap a pipe cleaner tightly around the middle and twist securely. Gently separate the tissue and fluff to make a rose.
3. Cut leaves from construction paper and tape or glue to the pipe cleaner stem.

Milagros

Materials
- tagboard
- aluminum foil
- pencil
- scissors
- toothpick
- tape
- permanent markers (optional)

Directions
1. Cut a mitten or heart shape from the tagboard. Cover with aluminum foil.
2. Use a toothpick to gently inscribe details and your name on the milagro. Decorate with marker.
3. Tape to the wall of the classroom.

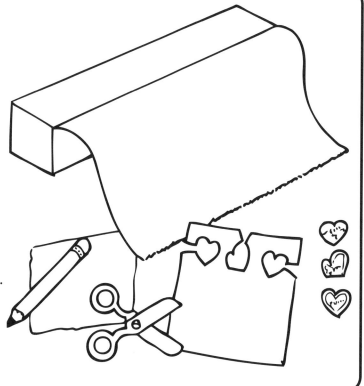

Los Reyes Magos

Children in Mexico do not usually receive their gifts on Christmas Day. On the evening of January 5, children set out their shoes with a note to *Los Reyes Magos*, or the Wise Men, telling them what they want. According to religious belief, it was the Wise Men who brought gifts to the baby Jesus on this day over 2,000 years ago.

The next day, families share *rosca*, a sweet bread made in the shape of a large doughnut. It contains a tiny porcelain doll made to represent the baby Jesus. The person who finds it must host another party before February 2, which is another holiday known as *Candelaria* (Candlemas). This day signifies the end of the holiday season in Mexico.

For the Teacher

Project

Celebrate Los Reyes Magos by making and eating holiday cakes.

Materials

- cupcake mix
- baking cups
- aluminum foil

Directions

1. Make cupcake batter as package directs. Twist a piece of aluminum foil into the shape of an infant. Drop it into one of the cups of batter. Bake as directed.

2. Instruct students not to bite directly into their cupcakes, but to first pull them apart to see if they have the "infant" in their cupcake. Give the person who finds it a new cupcake to eat.

3. The person who finds the doll in his or her cupcake becomes its padrino or madrina (godparent) and must bring in a treat for the class!

EP073 Mexico © Highsmith® Inc. 2007

Literature List

Ask your librarian for other book recommendations on Mexico.

The Aztec News
by Phillip Steele. Candlewick Press, 2000. 32 p. Gr. 4–6
Large-format, newspaper-style book with history, local news, witty ads, and tongue-in-cheek accounts.

Borreguita and the Coyote: A Tale from Ayutla
by Verna Aardema. Dragonfly, 1998. 32 p. Gr. 2–4
A trickster tale in which a little lamb uses her clever wiles to keep a coyote from eating her up.

Cinco de Mayo
by Alice K. Flanagan. Compass Point Books, 2003. 32 p. Gr. 3–5
Explores the history, customs, and symbols of Cinco de Mayo. Learn how Cinco de Mayo has changed over time and the different ways it is celebrated.

Cuckoo: A Mexican Folktale/Cucú: un cuento folklorico mexicano
by Lois Ehlert, translated by Gloria de Aragon Andujar. Harcourt, 1997. 40 p. Gr. 2–4
This traditional Mayan tale tells how the cuckoo lost her beautiful feathers. Bilingual.

Food and Festivals: Mexico
by Linda Illsley. Raintree, 1999. 32 p. Gr. 3–6
Discusses some of the foods enjoyed in Mexico and describes special foods that are part of baptisms, weddings, Easter, the Day of the Dead, and Christmas. Includes recipes.

Frida: The Artist Who Painted Herself
by Margaret Frith. Grosset and Dunlap, 2003. 32 p. Gr. 3–5
Through original artwork by Tomie de Paola, a longtime fan of Frida Kahlo's work, and beautiful reproductions of Kahlo's paintings, this book explores the creative, imaginative world of Mexico's most celebrated female artist.

A Library for Juana: The World of Sor Juana Inez
by Pat Mora. Knopf, 2002. 40 p. Gr. 3–5
A biography of the seventeenth-century Mexican poet, learned in many subjects, who became a nun later in life.

Magic Windows/Ventanas mágicas
by Carmen Lomas Garza. Children's Book Press, 1999. 30 p. Gr. 3–6
Carmen Lomas Garza portrays her family's Mexican customs through cut-paper work. Bilingual. Pura Belpre Award for illustration, 2000.

Mexico in Pictures
by Janice Hamilton. Lerner Publishing Group, 2002. 80 p. rev. ed. Gr. 4–6
A historical and current look at Mexico, discussing the land, the government, the people, and the economy.

Pablo Remembers
by George Ancona. HarperCollins, 1993. 48 p. Gr. 3–6
During the three-day celebration of the Days of the Dead, a young Mexican boy and his family make elaborate preparations to honor the spirits of the dead. Also available in Spanish.

The Pot That Juan Built
by Nancy Andrews–Goebel. Lee & Low Books, 2002. 32 p. Gr. 3–5
A cumulative rhyme summarizes the life's work of renowned Mexican potter Juan Quezada. Additional information describes the process he uses to create his pots after the style of the Casas Grandes people. Pura Belpre Honor Book for illustration, 2004.

The Two Mountains: An Aztec Legend
by Eric A. Kimmel. Shen's Books, 2000. 32 p. Gr. 3–6
When two married gods disobey their orders and visit Earth, they are turned into mortals as punishment, and eventually become mountains.

Glossary

adobe—a mixture of clay and mud that is formed into bricks and allowed to dry; the finished bricks are used for building houses

Aztecs—a great civilization that established its empire near the modern-day site of Mexico City; their empire covered most of southern Mexico

charreada—a Mexican-style rodeo, including competitions in roping, horsemanship, and steer wrestling

charro suit—the national costume of Mexican men; it consists of a short jacket called a bolero and riding pants; the outfit is often blue, trimmed with gold or silver buttons, and is worn with a sombrero

el jarabe tapatío—Mexican Hat Dance, a lively traditional dance performed all over Mexico

fiesta—Mexican party or celebration

jai alai—a Mexican ball game in which a hard rubber ball is bounced against a high wall by players using a basketlike racquet; it is known as one of the fastest games in the world

macahuitl—a wooden sword used by Aztec warriors; it was edged with sharp pieces of volcanic glass

mariachi—a band made up of four to 10 strolling musicians, who sing and play horns, guitars, and violins

masa—a corn-based dough; it is used to make tamales, a traditional Mexican dish

Maya—civilization that developed in southern Mexico and in parts of Central America; they devised the most accurate calendar used up to modern times

mestizos—descendants of Spanish settlers who married native people when they came to Mexico

occidental—western

Olmec—the first major civilization to develop in Mexico; they lived on the southern edge of the Gulf of Mexico

oriental—eastern

papel picado—a traditional art form of Mexico, created by cutting paper into decorative designs

pictographs—system of writing that was used by the Aztecs; instead of letters, words were represented by pictures

piñata—a hollow container made of clay or papier mâché; it is usually shaped as an animal, covered with bits of colorful tissue and filled with candy and treats

scribes—priests who were trained as writers; scribes created the books left by the Aztec Empire

serape—blankets worn over the shoulder by men in Mexico

sombrero—wide-brimmed Mexican hat made of felt or straw

sur—south

telpuchcalli—boarding school where Aztec boys were sent to be trained as warriors

tlachtli—a game similar to basketball that has been played by people in Mexico since ancient times

vaquero—cowboy

Volcanic Axis—a series of volcanoes extending across the southern portion of Mexico

Zapotecs—native civilization that developed in Southern Mexico; they were fierce warriors, and they developed the first writing system in the Americas